INTRODUCTION

This book aims to help you organise your home learning and your revision programmes, so that achieve the best results possible at A-level (Adva..... AS-level (Advanced Supplementary). The key to success is proper preparation.

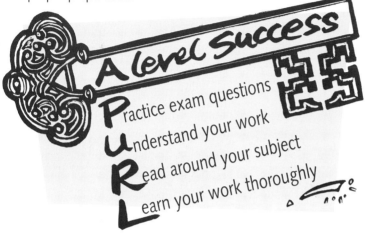

With all this groundwork done, you should be able to go into any examination room confident that you will do well.

STRUCTURE OF A- AND AS- LEVELS

There are two types of A- and AS- level syllabuses.

1. LINEAR

In this type of course you study for two years, after which time you will take written examinations plus, in some cases, coursework, practical assessments, orals etc. The AS course is half an A-level and can be taken after one year or, in some cases, as a safety net for A-level candidates who have found the course too difficult.

2. MODULAR

This type of course includes a 'core' which must be studied by every candidate. Candidates study several modules, depending upon the course, some of which may be core modules which are compulsory or some modules may contain core material. The core material may be examined in a 'synoptic' examination at the end of the course. In addition there will be several optional modules – fewer for AS than for A-level.

At the end of each module there is an examination which must be passed. The number of modules which must be taken may vary from subject to subject but a minimum number must be completed to qualify for a grade. Modular examinations may be repeated once if candidates are dissatisfied with their grades.

WHAT ABOUT A-LEVELS AND AS-LEVELS?

If you have not discovered already, you will soon find out that there is a world of difference between GCSE and Advanced level work.

At GCSE, you will have been required to learn a relatively small amount of factual information. You also needed to learn some fairly basic concepts and apply some of the information and concepts to unfamiliar situations.

Work for Advanced and Advanced Supplementary subjects has the same level of difficulty, but AS is, effectively, only half an A-level. For the rest of the book, they will both be referred to as A-level.

At A-level you may have only two, three or four subjects to cover but the *range* of material covered in those subjects is much more than at GCSE. You will need to do far more *learning* work, *understand advanced concepts*, and will have to *apply* both information and concepts using a level of skill which is far higher than any of those you used at GCSE. Remember, A-level is aimed at students who intend to continue into further study, leading to degrees from universities or to other higher professional qualifications. The work you do in the next two years prepares you for those courses.

It is crucial that you begin preparing for your A-level examinations as soon as possible after the start of the A-level course.

Unfortunately there are always a few students who believe that Y12 (also sometimes called the lower sixth year) is a rest year after GCSE! This year does offer many opportunities to develop interests other than what you will study formally, but to adopt the 'rest year' approach often leads to the lack of understanding of concepts and the lack of knowledge of important information which will be built upon in Y13. This, in turn, leads to stress, lack of progress and underachievement. Obviously, the result is disappointing A-level grades and the worry of whether or not it will be possible to get a place on a chosen course in higher education.

Of course, A-level years can be enjoyed, but they must also include a lot of very hard work. Make the most of these two years. Whilst being more difficult, A-level is far more interesting than the work you did at GCSE – you are really now beginning to study your chosen subjects in depth. Dive into some serious study!

SUPPORTED SELF-STUDY

Since A-level courses are long, teachers do not aim to spend a great deal of time on dealing with every tiny aspect of the course, and will expect you to participate in Supported Self-Study. You will now be expected to take notes during lessons and teachers will often give out 'hand-outs' which cover parts of the work, and advice on what to read up for yourself. This will often include references to your own text books and to other books or periodicals in the library. You may have timetabled study lessons in the library or in your subject department. During these times, your teacher should be there to help you study. Much of your remaining work will have to be done at home.

Here are a few tips to help you work more efficiently once you've got home at the end of each day:

Do organise your notes well and keep a clear index.

Do start each different topic on a new page and leave plenty of room for any additions you may make later.

Do make sure that headings are clear – underline or *highlight* important points.

Do read round your subject – using other text books or the references given by teachers.

Do supplement your notes with any additional information you may find in the references.

Do find information on a particular topic from as many sources as possible.

Do practice questions – they help you to assess your own understanding.

Don't be tempted to leave work until the weekend – you may well have forgotten some of it *and* new points may come up in the next lesson which requires a thorough understanding of today's lesson.

LEARNING

Supported Self-Study is all part of the learning process. Learning is long-term and builds on previous knowledge. Much of your A-level work will be new but it will build on the work you did at GCSE. Thorough learning of the new material as you meet it will help you to understand future work and will give you the depth of insight into the subject which is needed for Advanced level study. It will also make your work more interesting.

Be honest with yourself: you cannot cram A-level information into a few weeks of work. If you haven't understood topics and memorised information before you get to the revision stage you will spend your time in learning and not in revision. That is much harder and it takes a lot longer. Lay solid foundations and build upon your learning carefully and daily.

Learning is like in-putting and processing information on a computer. This information can be 'called up' at a later stage. Unfortunately, unlike a computer, our memory 'forgets' information if it is not used and refreshed regularly. For example, the French you learned while on holiday in France is soon forgotten if you don't use it when you return home. You will need to fix what you need to know in your memory through revision. Read on for some help with this.

REVISION

Revision is the process of refreshing your memory about things which you have already learned. Using the computer analogy, you need to be able to 'call up' information as and when it is needed. You also need to have easy access to what you have learned and understood. Revision helps you to store information in your long term memory, and helps your mind by

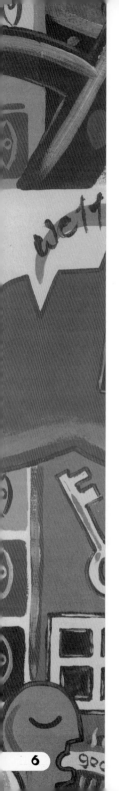

prompting the memory so that what you have learned can be used when needed, eg. when doing a problem or during an exam.

Revision helps you to organise, select and adapt what you have learned.

FIRST PRINCIPLES

Those of you who are studying science or maths-based subjects may very well have a large number of formulae etc. to absorb. Remember that in A-level exams, you will not always receive sheets of formulae or mathematical relationships. You must either learn them or work them out.

If you thoroughly understand your work you can save a lot of learning by working problems from first principles. You need not remember the formula or equation. You start by using the basic concepts and building on these using your knowledge rather than trying to remember a formula and then applying it. Initially, this may seem to be a fairly lengthy process but it can be done very quickly and can save a lot of time. It also means that you can apply concepts to unknown situations without having to worry about remembering several mathematical formulae. The advantages include not having to remember 'how to do' each kind of problem.

With practice, you can rapidly work out how to apply your knowledge to problems. A very useful technique which you can apply to many mathematical and scientific problems when you are not sure how to get started in a difficult situation is to invent a simpler one. A very simple example of this is converting °F to °C. The formula is:

$$°F = 9/5 \times °C + 32$$

Often it is difficult to remember which way round the equation works so just remember a simplified version i.e. $2 \times °C + 30$. This gives the clue of which way to work.

The simpler technique should contain the main features of the more complex – a good example is the Sine Rule. You may not remember that **a/SinA = b/SinB** for *any* triangle but you can quickly get the result from the *special case* of a right angled triangle using just your knowledge of the sine of an angle.

Work it out.

$$\text{Sin A} = \frac{a}{c}, \quad \text{Sin B} = \frac{b}{c}$$

$$\therefore \frac{a}{\text{Sin A}} = \frac{b}{\text{Sin B}} = c$$

(really c/Sin C but angle C = 90° so Sin C = 1)

This is a very basic example, but it shows how the fundamental concepts of trigonometry can be used to produce a formula quickly and easily without having to remember anything but the main rules.

WHEN TO START LEARNING

You have been learning all your life but now you have to bridge the gap between GCSE and A-level. It is essential that you start learning for A-level right at the start of the course. You may be surprised by the sheer quantity of work you will need to cover. Sort out what are the most important points to learn and establish patterns which will help you to 'hang on' to facts.

There are no short cuts to success at A-level. Hard work and commitment over a long period of time are essential

ingredients. This is far more important now than it ever was when you were working towards GCSE.

You will learn much more – and more easily if you:

★ **Do make sure that you understand new concepts – if in doubt, ASK.** Never leave something you don't understand in the hope that it will go away, it won't. Teachers are only too willing to help you understand and will help you all they can.

★ **Do discuss and try to explain new ideas and concepts with a friend.** This helps you both to understand. Explaining something is a very good test of understanding because you have to begin from basic ideas.

★ **Do make sure that homework is done thoroughly.** Homework consolidates lessons, it helps you to understand new concepts and helps you memorise information. If you don't do homework, read round your subject, annotate your notes or practice questions you will find it hard to achieve the grade you really want.

★ **Do develop ways of committing information to memory.** Be an active learner. Writing notes or reading out loud helps you to concentrate. Make lists of important points. Having gone over a topic, try to repeat the work without your book. Keep doing this until you can remember all aspects of the topic easily.

WHEN TO START REVISING

If you are studying a modular A-level, some Examination Boards examine most of all of the core syllabus in the form of a 'synoptic' examination at the end of the course. Others examine parts of the core in individual modules. Check your syllabus to find out what you have to do. If you are required to take a separate synoptic examination you must at least revise **all** the **core** modules for this exam.

Once you have completed an examination for an optional module you need not revise the work for that module again unless you decide to re-sit because you were dissatisfied with your grade.

It is important to realise that you can enjoy life and revise at the same time. Revision need not be the drudge that it appears, but it does need determination and planning. There are several important points to remember about effective revision. Most important of all is that revision is not something that is done the night before an exam. If you spread the work load over a longer period you:

- are likely to achieve more
- will be under a lot less pressure and enjoy your work more
- are less likely to experience stress, strain, panic and underachievement
- will have more time to relax, to keep fit and to enjoy life.

You should begin serious revision for final A-level examinations at least 12 weeks before the first exam.

For individual modules in a modular style A-level, you should begin your revision about 6–7 weeks before each exam. If you start later than this you can still succeed but it will be more difficult because you will have less time to revise.

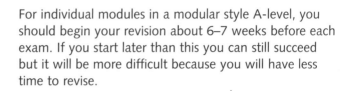

PLANNING YOUR WORK

Do find out the dates of your exams: don't forget orals, practical exams, etc.

Do draw up a revision timetable. The time for this is early March for final exams.

Do divide your time into weekly programmes for March, April and May and don't forget weekends.

Do review weaknesses which might have been highlighted by the mock exams and allocate additional time during your schedule for these areas.

Do plan to do some revision *every day* – about one hour per subject – in at least two subjects. This should be increased at weekends to around three hours per subject, but remember that your concentration span is unlikely to be more than 30 minutes so remember to take regular breaks.

Do get into the habit of revising at set times. Some people get up early, others revise better in the evening or during the early hours. Find out which is best for you.

Do make sure that you have a quiet place in which you can work undisturbed.

Do arrange to have regular breaks – five to ten minutes every half hour. During the breaks do something you particularly enjoy. It will give you something to look forward to, especially if the work is hard going.

Don't try to work with a radio, TV or CD etc. playing. Your mind will concentrate far better if you have peace and quiet and are not distracted. Ask people *not* to bring coffee or disturb you because your concentration will be broken.

NB – The above criteria also apply to modular examinations which take place, for example, in January/February. Your revision time-table should be started in October.

PLANNING YOUR WORK

A revision plan is a vital element of your schedule. Not only will it help you to remember what you have to do, it will remind you of what you have already done: this boosts confidence and helps to reduce stress. A plan will also help to ensure that all work is covered at least once and that the areas in which you have experienced difficulties can be emphasised.

A little time spent planning in March or October can save you a great deal of time and worry later on.

- Use the timetable on the next page to help you – you may make as many copies as you wish. Use one page for every week between now and the first exam.
- Divide each day into 30 minute sessions with a break of five minutes between some and ten minutes between others. Remember to mark in mealtimes and be realistic about how long you can keep going. Twelve hours per day – even if you are behind with your work – is way over the top.
- Set aside some time every day for relaxation – perhaps an hour each evening during the week and on Saturday or Sunday afternoons. A Saturday night out would not go amiss but remember, no very late nights – you have work to do the next day.

Write down all your commitments including:
- lesson times
- school/college activities – matches, rehearsals, clubs and societies

- other activities – part-time job, venture scouts, etc.
- times for relaxation and enjoyment

If time is short and you have a lot to do, you will need to drop some activities in order to make up time. This may be difficult, but it will only be for a few weeks.

WHEN AND WHAT TO REVISE

Remember to find out the time of day which best suits you to revise. Even during school days time should be set aside every day for revision. Plan to:

- do your regular homework – this is a must
- revise, in addition to homework, at least two subjects per day for about one hour each
- get into a routine which you can cope with easily.

If you are taking General Studies, take more of an interest in what is going on around the world and read widely, particularly good quality newspapers.

TOP TIPS FOR PLANNING

Do find out when your teachers will complete the courses.

Do go through each of your exam syllabuses and list topics which you know you understand properly, topics which you are uncertain about and topics which you definitely don't understand. This should give you a realistic idea of what you have to do.

Do write down a list of deadlines for handing in essential work – essays, assignments, practical assessments etc.

Do ensure that during your revision period you allocate enough time to revise each topic several times – this will refresh your memory and you will remember more each time you revise the work. Remember, several short bursts are better than one long effort.

Do make sure that you cover every topic at least once if you are late in starting your revision.

- **Do** leave some time during the final week of revision to cover topics which have been particularly difficult.
- **Do** build in a variety of topics into a revision session. The brain works better if you cover several different topics during your revision sessions, rather than just one.
- **Do** divide each topic into manageable parts so that you don't try to do too much at one session.

RECOGNISING AND BEATING STRESS

Even though a little stress can be good for you, excessive stress can be very harmful and should be avoided.

There are many reasons why students experience stress. These include loneliness, guilt, fear of failure, pressure from parents and teachers to do well, pressure from universities to obtain particular grades or just trying to cope with too many things at once. People suffering from stress are usually easily recognisable.

emotional and very sensitive

depression, no self-esteem

short-tempered, irritable

can't sleep, wakes early and worries

headaches, not hungry, skin problems

wants to be alone

can't concentrate

Not only are these symptoms unpleasant, they can be very harmful. If you have one or more of these symptoms your revision and exam performance can be adversely affected.

Here are some strategies which could help you cope with stressful periods.

Establish a routine and stick to it. Ensure that you eat properly, get enough sleep and keep to your work plan.

Start revising as soon as possible. The later you leave the start of your revision, the more you will have to do in a shorter period of time.

Take regular breaks. Remember that your concentration is better in short bursts.

Attempt as many past papers and questions as possible. Practising past papers helps you to know what to expect and to find out what extras you might have to read. The more you do the less likely you are to be caught out.

Build in variety. Revising several subjects for short periods each and varying your break time activities helps to reduce stress.

Seek company. Make sure that you see friends regularly. You can even share your problems with them.

Do your best. You can do no more than this. If others brag about how much they have done don't listen to them. Decide what works for you and stick to it.

Ignore panic. Panic is catching and leads to extra stress. Relax regularly. Try the exercise described below.

RELAXATION EXERCISE

Find a comfortable place, lie down and close your eyes. Tense all your muscles, clench fists, really make every muscle tense. Now deliberately relax each muscle one at a time until you are completely still. Breathe in deeply. Hold your breath for a count of 5. Breathe out gently.

Repeat this, listening to your breath, for a couple of minutes. If thoughts enter your head, just let them go. Concentrate only on your breathing. Now that you are relaxed, enjoy the peace and quiet. Enjoy the feeling of stress melting away.

SIX TIPS FOR EFFECTIVE REVISION

1. PREPARE YOUR WORKPLACE

Everyone needs an undisturbed place to work in which they are comfortable and private. If you have your own room, make sure that you have:

- a comfortable chair which supports your back properly
- a table which has enough room for you to work and which is by a window
- a table lamp which gives plenty of light
- all the books you need
- pens, pencils, paper
- a tidy work area.

If you cannot find a quiet place to work in you own home, see if you can find a quiet spot in the local library or in the school library – perhaps your teachers might be able to help.

2. LEARNING BY HEART

Exams are designed to test several things, including what you know, what you understand and how well you can interpret new information using what you have learned and understood.

If you practice doing past papers and listen carefully to what your teachers have to say you will soon know what you should 'learn by heart'. Writing notes and drawing diagrams also help you to understand your work and to

memorise it. Here is a reminder of what might be worth learning by heart for A-level:

- ✪ connections between facts and patterns which give shape to a topic, eg. – definitions, scientific laws, stages in a chemical process, historical events
- ✪ vocabulary in whichever foreign language you are learning
- ✪ quotations from literature which support statements you may want to make
- ✪ diagrams or drawings – say – of science apparatus you may have to draw
- ✪ scientific facts such as chemical formulae – if you are taking chemistry
- ✪ mathematical formula – etc.

3. ACTIVE LEARNING

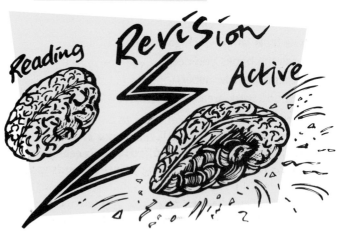

By the time you begin A-level courses, you know that reading on its own is not enough if you are to revise effectively. Your learning needs to be stimulated by activities which will help to prevent your mind from wandering and help you to learn. You can stimulate your mind by:

- ✪ **writing** down important points in note form

- ✪ **drawing** diagrams two or three times or making flow charts from a list of points
- ✪ **testing** yourself by covering a drawing etc. and drawing it without the book, then checking it
- ✪ **reading out loud** and allowing your own voice to stimulate your memory
- ✪ **underlining** interesting points or quotations, then writing them down until you can remember them
- ✪ **making up word games** or mnemonics to help you, eg. ROYGBIV for the visible spectrum (Red, Orange, Yellow, Green, Blue, Indigo, Violet)
- ✪ **explaining** topics to another person, because to explain something you must both know it and understand it
- ✪ **persuading** someone to test you on what you have learned
- ✪ **working** through past exam papers.

4. REVISION NOTES

Taking notes during lessons is very important. Make sure that all your notes are well spaced and have headings, sub-headings and numbered points. Your notes will be easier to read, understand and remember.

When you come to revise it is important that you look at your notes again and amend them as necessary so that they can be shortened. Putting points on cards (post-cards) would be helpful. Make sure that you revise using the patterns of each topic to help you. Lists are very helpful when you are reducing or 'patterning' notes. They are particularly good if you number the points in your list, eg. listing the seven characteristics of living things or number the factors which led up to an historical event.

More highly patterned examples might include:

What happens next? A chronological list or sequence of events leading up to a battle or in the plot of a novel;

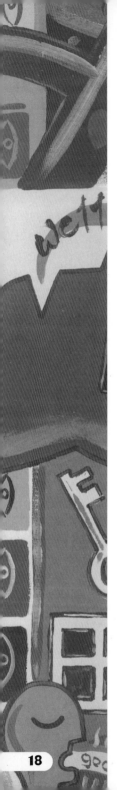

What happens next and why? Cause and effect. Try and see facts as a chain of linked ideas, eg. changing ice into steam.

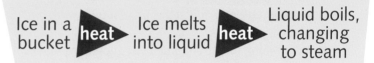

Ice in a bucket **heat** Ice melts into liquid **heat** Liquid boils, changing to steam

Arguments. These will always have two sides. Often, one side will be in favour and the other against a viewpoint; problems often have more than one possible solution; proposals usually have advantages and disadvantages. It might be useful to draw up a table – for and against – on opposite sides of a page.

Comparing Capital Punishment with Life-imprisonment

Capital Punishment	Life Imprisonment
Final	Not final
No possibility of reprieve after event, if mistake has been made	Possible to reprieve with new evidence
Cheap to taxpayer	Expensive to taxpayer
Punishment only	Punishment and rehabilitation
Mercy not shown	Mercy shown

Similarities and differences. Again, a table detailing similarities and differences can be drawn on a page.

Diagrams, flowcharts and tables. All of these can help to reduce the amount you have to read and so make revision easier. They also help when you're planning answers in the exam, because the memory stores and recalls 'pictures' more easily than words.

5. MEMORY BOOSTERS

It is often easier to remember shapes and pictures than to remember words. Usually, if you remember one bit of a pattern or chain, this triggers the memory and the brain does the rest.

You will remember things better if you make up your own patterns. However, if you find that difficult or if time is very short, Revision Notes, Study Guides or Key facts – are available. They do some of the work for you.

You might find that drawing pictures and sticking them round the room is helpful. It is amazing how often the eye 'catches' them. Each time it does, your memory is jogged. In this way, you can revise without even trying! When it comes to the exam, you may well be able to picture the card on the door with the pattern you need. It's there, in your memory, ready for use. Sometimes a striking mental image will jog your memory – especially if it is funny or rude. The funnier the better.

Some people remember best through the use of word association. Using initial letters, for instance, can be very helpful memory joggers. Some examples are shown below:

Word Association. Stalactites and Stalagmites: tights come down and mites grow up. (In this case you could also use c from ceiling and g from ground).

Musical keys with sharps.

	Go	Down	And	Enter	By	Force	Charlie
key	g	d	a	e	b	f#	c#
sharps	1	2	3	4	5	6	7

Rhymes. Winds blow from high to low.

You can memorise all sorts of things using these tricks. It's worthwhile finding the memory boosters which work for you: they really help.

6. PRACTISING EXAM QUESTIONS

Practising A-level questions is a vital part of your preparation for the exams. Before you start to answer practice questions it is essential that you have thoroughly revised your notes. Trying to answer questions having done little work in that topic will cause a lot of unnecessary stress. There are several styles of exam questions. They are designed to test your ability in three key skill areas.

Most teachers will give you past papers to do for home-work. This is a real advantage because your teacher will mark the paper and go through it with you. Not only do you find out how well you have done but you also hear about how better to tackle questions. Do as many past papers as possible – they are *always* beneficial.

SELECT – Only relevant and important points relating to the questions

COMBINE – Points from different areas of a topic, or from different topics

INTERPRET – Ability to interpret unseen information using what you know to help you

KEY SKILL AREAS TESTED BY A-LEVEL QUESTIONS

Working through past papers improves your sense of:

Timing. Work out how much time you have to do each question and try to keep to the time limit – this will help to reduce any feelings of panic in the actual exam.

Planning. Make brief answer plans for long essay questions. All you need is a list of your main headings and key points. Your teacher will provide guidance about where and how marks are to be gained.

Recognising styles of question. Familiarise yourself with the different ways examiners ask questions.

THE EXAMS

It is very tempting to continue with revision right up to the last moment, and even between exams. You can get that nagging, guilty, feeling that you could do just that little bit extra. But, like an athlete who times his or her physical peak to coincide with the athletics event, you should consider yourself approaching *your* peak.

By the week before the first exam, you should be easing off. Too much now may mean that you reach your peak too soon. There is little point in going into an exam exhausted, fed up and burnt out. You'll never be able to do your best. If you work right up to the last minute all the topics will be churning about in your mind and you

will probably find that you can't remember some of them. This is very likely to cause sleeplessness and unnecessary stress at a time when you least need it. Take time out before each exam. As a result, you will be fresh and able to use your memory and mind to the best of your ability.

DURING THE WEEK BEFORE THE EXAMS:

- make sure that you get plenty of exercise and sleep
- refresh your memory on a few of the difficult of essential points
- catch up if you have fallen behind, but don't overdo it.

THE NIGHT BEFORE AN EXAM

Don't be tempted to do any work for tomorrow's exam. Additional work could make you forget more than you have learned. Totally relax, do something you really enjoy doing.

At this stage, don't compare notes with friends. If one of your friends is stressed and depressed, this is likely to rub off on you. However well prepared you are, a friend's panic can be catching. Relax by yourself instead.

It is fairly likely that, however hard you try, you will not be able to stop thinking about the exam – particularly if it's the first one. There are things which you can do which will help. Sort out practical details before the morning. Here's a checklist to help with this:

- make sure that you have all your exam equipment ready – pen and spares, pencil, pencil sharpener, rubber, ruler and other items which you may be allowed to take into the exam, such as a calculator. Put them in your bag, ready for the morning.
- Check your exam timetable – which room is the exam in? Check the time you have to be there.
- Have a warm bath and, afterwards, try the relaxation exercises described on page 15.

- ✪ Go to bed early, and you should be able to sleep!!
- ✪ Don't drink alcohol or take sleeping pills. They will dull your brain for the following day.

IN THE EXAM ROOM

Everybody who goes into an exam room has a churning stomach. Take heart, you are not the only one! It is important that you relax as much as possible before you look at the exam paper.

TOP TIPS TO REMOVE BUTTERFLIES!!

Do get out all the equipment that you will need for this exam and arrange it on your desk.

Do take your watch off and check the time against the exam room clock. Put it on your desk so that you can easily see it.

Do fill in the relevant sections on the front of your examination script.

Do read your exam paper with care. Make sure that you read the instructions and underline important points. Are there any compulsory questions? Make sure you understand fully what you need to do.

Do read the exam paper twice over. Ten minutes now can save a lot of time later. Your brain will already be working on those difficult questions, and you'll avoid making mistakes.

Do underline important words on your exam paper. What does the examiner want? What topics are involved?

Do work out how much time you have for each question. It's a good idea to mark the time a question should be finished on the paper.

Do boost you own confidence by deciding which question you can do best and doing it first.

Do make sure that you have at least five minutes at the end of the exam to go over what you have done. It is

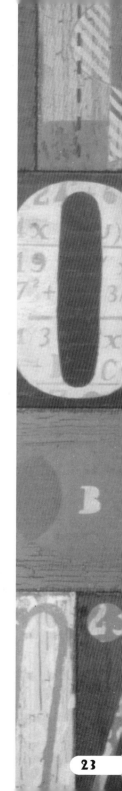

amazing how many marks can be picked up just by quickly going through your script and adding points you had missed.

Don't panic if your mind appears to go blank. Once you start answering questions, your memory will start to work again. Look at key words in the question to help you.

Don't waste time thinking and worrying about losing an odd mark in part of a difficult question, when you could gain several marks by going onto the next one. Leave it and come back to it later, if you have time.

GET ALL THE MARKS YOU DESERVE HINTS FOR HELPING WITH ESSAY QUESTIONS

Essay questions test knowledge *and* your ability to organise ideas into sentences and sections. These need to make coherent and lucid prose.

Planning is vital. Before you start writing an essay, spend a few minutes planning what you wish to say. Make brief notes on the following:

The introduction. This gives the examiner a very brief summary of your response to the question, and how you will organise your assay accordingly. If you do not finish, it may well give the examiner some information for which marks can be given.

Headings. These are the points about which you are going to write.

Key words and brief notes. These are the notes you will use when you write the essay proper. Key words will help jog your memory.

Paragraphs. Each new idea should be in a new paragraph. Remember to include examples of each point you make and use quotation marks when quoting direct speech, etc.

The conclusion. This short section enables you to sum up your ideas at the end.

TOP TIP

When you have finished your plan, write your essay as precisely and concisely as you can. Then neatly cross out the rough notes you have made. Make sure that you re-read what you have written. You may be able to spot – and rectify – the odd mistake, or add bits which could gain you extra marks.

HINTS ON DISCUSSION QUESTIONS

Introduction. A short section in which you indicate how you will tackle the main body of the question.

Discussion section. The main section. Make points for and points against. Each point needs to be backed up with evidence.

Conclusion. This is the section in which you sum up the most important aspects of the discussion. Be logical – use the evidence you have given to arrive at a conclusion which fits the evidence.

MATHS AND SCIENCE QUESTIONS

Past papers are essential – the more practice you have in doing maths and science problems the better. Practice helps you to know how to tackle questions, how to begin answering them and what concepts you need to know. It also helps you to learn how to use the 'first principle' approach.

Often maths and science questions ask you to prove something. If you are asked to show or prove that A = B, you must use your *knowledge* of A to prove that it equals B. Obviously, you will lose marks if you try to prove that B = A. Similarly, you will lose marks if you prove that if A = C and that B = C, then it is reasonable to assume that A = B, since both equal C. The reason for the loss in marks is that you have not carried out the examiner's instructions. He or she required you to prove that A = B. Do just that.

SCIENCE ESSAY QUESTIONS

In science questions which involve essays, marks are awarded for sound arguments backed up by factual information and evidence. Again, planning is important. Think carefully about what you want to say, sequence your points and provide evidence.

For example, if a question asks you to discuss the trends of the periodic table by reference to oxides, you *must* keep to oxides in order to gain your marks.

The following could be part of a physics question:

> *Explain why the sun is redder at sunset and appears to be larger than at midday.*

To answer this, ask yourself what the examiner wishes to know.

There are two main parts. Firstly, why the sun appears to be bigger at sunset and, secondly, why it appears redder at sunset.

Now make a numbered list of the main points of your answer. Keep them logical, accurate and brief:

Main Points

1. At sunset, the sun is nearer to the horizon, so light has further to travel than at midday.

2. Water vapour in the air magnifies. At sunset, light passes through more water vapour, hence greater magnification at sunset. The result is that the sun appears larger.

3. Light is 'scattered' by particles in air. Blue light is scattered more than red light. Less blue light than red light gets through, therefore the sun appears redder.

ARTS SUBJECTS REQUIRING LONGER ESSAY ANSWERS

Practice in past papers is also vital in subjects such as English and History. Revise a topic, then answer questions related to it. In English, examiners read your answers and then use the mark band which best fits the overall quality. They mark what they have read, so you must:

- be positive with answers
- be methodical and accurate
- make a range of valid points
- develop points which include your interpretation of texts
- whenever possible, show how close to the text you are working by using quotations as evidence for your points.

If you are studying English, you will need to develop skills in critical appreciation. This involves analysis and interpretation when reading new passages of prose or poetry in an exam. Read unseen passages two or three

times, making notes and underlining important points. In the second or third reading, try to recognise meanings, feelings, moods, atmosphere, emotions and links between one part of the text and another. Bear in mind the author's intentions when writing, and his or her intended audience.

Most exam boards are looking for the following skills in critical appreciation:

- ⊙ an ability to respond with understanding to texts
- ⊙ an ability to discuss your own and other readers' interpretations of the text
- ⊙ independent and informed judgements
- ⊙ clear communication of knowledge and understanding
- ⊙ an ability to explore layers of meaning in texts
- ⊙ an appreciation of features such as argument, character and imagery
- ⊙ an ability to show how tests might excite specific emotions.

ORAL EXAMS

Oral exams such as those needed for Modern Languages, are always daunting but if you have prepared well in advance, you needn't worry. You are very likely to use what you have prepared. The examiner will try to put you at your ease on the day.

The major differences between a speaking test and a written exam are that you meet the examiner and you have little chance to correct errors. If you make a mistake, therefore, correct it as soon as you realise. It's not a good idea to try to correct mistakes if you realise later on. You may lose the thread, and marks, if you try to backtrack.

In oral tests marks are awarded for *accent, accuracy and content* and for *range of language used*. Here are some hints to help your test to go smoothly:

Do make sure that you know what to do and how long each section lasts.

Do find out what notes you can use and what period of preparation is given in the exam itself.

Do read newspapers, watch TV news, discuss items with friends and clarify your opinions.

Do jot down – in French, German, Spanish, etc. – some key vocabulary. Make up some sentences that express your views on a subject which can be used for general conversation. This is your chance to show off your up-to-date knowledge.

Do have some original ideas to talk about. Prepare these before the test.

Do prepare evidence to back up your ideas.

Do listen to the question and answer the question you are asked.

Do react positively to the examiner's questions and comments.

Do take a moment or two to think about an answer. The use, for example, of '*Alors, bon*' gives time for you to think and helps prevent prepared answers from sounding rehearsed.

Don't hesitate, as slow, hesitant speech will lose marks.

WORDS USED BY EXAMINERS

Check out these words – they're all used by examiners. How sure are you of their meanings?

calculate – this means that a numerical answer is needed – remember to show your working.

complete – you must complete a sentence, drawing, table, graph, etc.

define – describe precisely.

describe – a series of important points must be written down in a few sentences.

explain – write down what you understand – sometimes, particularly in science, a diagram helps.

find – this term is often used in maths and may mean that you have to do a calculation, make a reading from a graph or take a measurement.

outline – brief notes are needed about only the most important points.

predict – use some given information or information which you have found to say what is likely to happen as a result.

state – a brief answer giving basic facts is needed.

suggest – this often refers to information or a situation which is not on the syllabus but you will have been given information in the question which you can use. There may be more than one answer.

Finally, keep your examiner happy!

- ☸ produce neat, legible work
- ☸ use standard English at all times in your answers
- ☸ avoid shorthand and using 'etc'.

The examiner is on your side. He or she wants to give you the marks if at all possible, but you have to earn them.

WHAT TO DO BETWEEN EXAMS

Only revise points which are particularly important or you are not absolutely sure about for the following day's exam. Remember to take the night off for relaxation and rest before an exam the next day. Eat plenty and get a good night's sleep.

Although it is tempting, try not to discuss the last exam with friends and certainly don't do a 'post mortem' on it. Everybody thinks that they haven't done as well as they really have, so talking about it will only make you depressed and cause stress which will make you less confident for the next examination.

ONCE THE EXAMS ARE OVER

Let your hair down and party – you deserve it! The important thing now is not to worry – there is little point in worrying about something you cannot change. Whilst everybody knows that good exam results are important, they are not the ultimate decider of your future. The worst that can happen if you don't get the grades you hoped for is that you may have to re-sit some subjects or amend your plans. Look up other

similar courses which might require lower grades. Ask for careers advisors and UCAS to help if necessary.

Be positive – go into each exam thinking about passing with good grades. Never go into an exam afraid that you might fail. After all, you've worked hard, so you deserve a good grade!

GOOD LUCK!!

Be Positive

First published 1998, Reprinted 2000 (twice)
Letts Educational
Schools and Colleges Division
9-15 Aldine Street
London W12 8AW
020 8740 2266
e-mail: mail@lettsed.co.uk

Text:© Alan Brewerton

Design and illustrations © Letts Educational Ltd 1998

Design, page layout and illustration by Hart McLeod, Cambridge

British Library Cataloguing-in-Publication Data

A CIP record for this book is available from the British Library

ISBN 1 84085 080 9

Printed in Great Britain by Ashford Colour Press

Letts Educational Ltd, a division of Granada Learning Ltd.
Part of the Granada Media Group.